Twenty Questions

poems by

John Delaney

Finishing Line Press
Georgetown, Kentucky

Twenty Questions

Copyright © 2019 by John Delaney
ISBN 978-1-63534-969-6 First Edition
All rights reserved under International and Pan-American Copyright Conventions. No part of this book may be reproduced in any manner whatsoever without written permission from the publisher, except in the case of brief quotations embodied in critical articles and reviews.

ACKNOWLEDGMENTS

Grateful appreciation is due the editors of the following magazines where some of the poems first appeared:

The Blue Moon Literary & Art Review: "The Blue Wire"
La Concha (Newsletter of American Pilgrims on the Camino): "Finisterre"
Dash Literary Journal: "Obitus Canis"
Poetry Super Highway: "1956"
Roanoke Review: "Afterwards / After Words", "Only Child"
Still Point Arts Quarterly: "Leaves"
Visitant: "Fashion Designer", "Paper Wasps", "Purple Finch"
Vox Poetica: "Penny Thoughts"

Publisher: Leah Maines
Editor: Christen Kincaid
Author Photo: Evelyn van Naerssen
Cover Design: Elizabeth Maines McCleavy

Printed in the USA on acid-free paper.
Order online: www.finishinglinepress.com
also available on amazon.com

Author inquiries and mail orders:
Finishing Line Press
P. O. Box 1626
Georgetown, Kentucky 40324
U. S. A.

Table of Contents

1956 1

Obitus Canis 2

Only Child 3

Afterwards /After Words 4

The Blue Wire 5

Finisterre (Galicia, Spain) 6

Purple Finch 8

World Enough and Time 9

The Seagull's Cry 10

Eulogy for My Body 11

Aste<u>risk</u> 19

Fashion Designer 20

Paper Wasps 21

Donations and Gifts 23

Penny Thoughts 24

Graybeard 25

Heron Waiting 26

In Sickness and In Health 27

Leaves 28

Dividing by Zero 29

To Evelyn and Andrew,
Answers

"Were we called upon to give one piece of advice and
only one to young beginners in this game,
it would be 'Don't be afraid of asking questions?' . . .
Real or imaginary? Tangible or intangible? Is it now existing?
What are its uses? Whom does it instruct? . . . "

—from *Twenty Questions: A Short Treatise
on the Game* (1882) by Hotspur

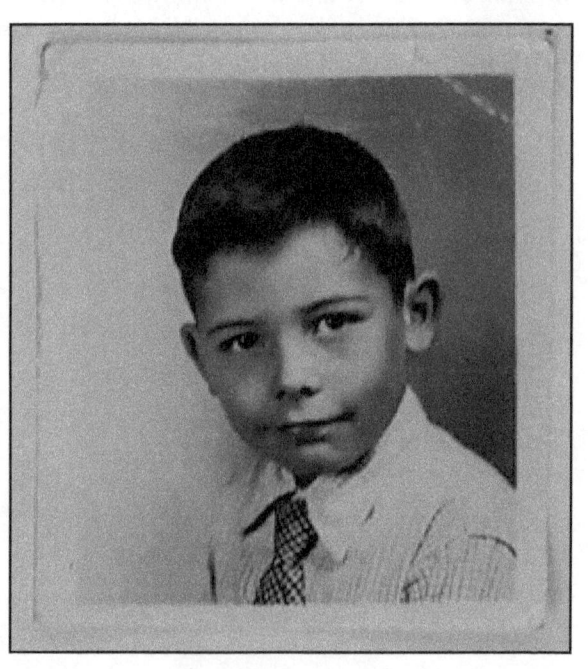

1956

I hardly recognize the little boy
I was in the kindergarten
graduation photo.
Wearing a plaid tie
and a lightly checkered
short-sleeve shirt,
sporting a butch haircut.
He faces the camera, but looks beyond:
the future calling like a playground
with its swings, seesaw, and jungle gym.
Waiting to rush away
to raucous play in the dirt.
Wanting another turn on the slide.
God-like, I know everything
that would happen after,
the ups and downs, cuts and scrapes and hurt.
Pushing off, learning to hold tight,
not looking down or back.
Though it's not a question
he could answer then,
nor am I better able now—
but still I wonder often:
did I become the man
I should have been?

Obitus Canis

What can you learn from an old dog you loved?

That food is a reason to jump for joy at any time.
That morning can never come early enough.
Never to shun a stranger at your door,
nor stop fawning over your friends.
To follow your nose to the source.
The contagion of enthusiasm.
A companionable silence.
How devoted subjects train their masters.

True to your breed, now you run to fetch
something that's irretrievable.

Only Child

No one to remember who you were, when.
No one to conspire with against us.
No one to take the fall now and then,
or later, even, foil our consensus.

No one to show you up or hold you back.
No one to divide our hugs and kisses.
No one to contest y(our) will in probate, Jack,
nor keep you to your promises.

While science with its test-tube magic might
have offered us another choice, or chance,
its moonlit logic never reached romance:
we adopted this role in the daylight.

Now we've put all our eggs in your basket:
sunny-side up, deviled, soft and hard boiled.
That some are likely to get broken or spoiled
there is no question—so we don't ask it.

Afterwards / After Words

I thought of a car
left in a lot
with its headlights on,
unnoticed all day
till the dark
became the backdrop
to shine—
while its energy
drained,
dimmed,
died.
What would it take
to jump-start
this heart?

The Blue Wire

How the mouse knew
I could do
without the blue wire
will make folklore
in rodentia.

So far
the car
starts and runs
with no perceptible
loss of function.

Synapses
cease and desist
every day, they say,
but the brain
feels no pain

yet. Yet you wonder
how the thing
operates under
the hood
now with less—

if dementia
could be a ruse
to defuse
the mind's
time bomb.

Finisterre (Galicia, Spain)

The dream brings you to the end of the world.
What more could you have wanted than this bar,
serving *vino tinto* and *raciones*,
while throngs of people share a photo op?

Had you thought that everything would stop
when the path ended? Many hearts leapt off
the edge watching the sun set, dissolving
upon the dark water, splaying out

its colors in broad bands. That is when doubt
must have crept into the consciousness
of those seeking to worship its radiance,
to where it was rising in splendor again.

Every age is an ignorant one. Such men
sail like Columbus from Gomera,
venture forth like Magellan from Seville,
not knowing what everyone one day will.

But still . . . when we walked down the hill
back to Fisterra, in the gradual dark,
a full moon began its rise across the bay,
offering a coincident change of light

that turned everything into black or white.
Content with what we know, most of us
will stay at home, leave adventuring
to the reckless, rich, and irredeemers,

and live our lives out simply as dreamers.
We'll spare ourselves the disappointments
and the injuries, all that prep time,
and fulfill our fantasies with headlines.

Yet men want to follow where the sun shines.
Myriads over millenia
have sat on those rocks where we had been,
mesmerized by the meaning of that view—

perhaps with a drink of wine, as we did too—
but deprived of the common knowledge
that takes so much for granted now, and makes
a wondrous sunset feel like *déjà-vu*.

Purple Finch

Your head is the size of a small acorn.
You barely weigh more than a first-class letter.
Hard to imagine—out of an egg born—
from the get-go, you were a go-getter.

So much to see and do within each minute!
Branches were your brethren. Your rosy vest
flashing among them trailed a warbling fest.
Sunflower seeds fueled your frantic diet.

The world is an adventure, full of harm,
but made more precious from your visit.
In my hand, your still body still is warm—
yet you are gone, and all that goes with it.

Fancy the flights if you had not flown
where a cat would enforce its no-fly zone.

World Enough and Time

First things first: the Big Bang
that began the universe.
A scattershot
of something into
what was not.

Centrifugal eons
gathering galaxies
in swirls like icing.
Even then, one might say,
we were on the way.

Evolutionary eras
ratcheting up
the primordial wheel.
Already in the mix of things
matter began to feel.

Interminable periods
field-testing Tyrannosaurus
and Triceratops
and countless forms before us
to reach a state of mind.

Epochs and ages
have come and gone
perfecting the process.
Life orbits on
into the future.

Fished from teeming time,
love was our lure.
Why did it take so long
to find each other?
We had to be sure.

The Seagull's Cry

Is it that the sea has left the shore
and you are calling it home?
So raucous in your voice:
the tide creeps in on foam.

Is it that the sun will shine no more
and you are lost on your perch?
So quarrelsome in your choice:
the sunrise solves your search.

Is it your impatience to soar
in the wind above the waves?
So overwrought, you rejoice,
shrieking what your spirit craves.

Eulogy for My Body

One thing I know: you'll be the death of me.
So let me have my say while I am able.
I won't be around when they come for you.

Like a proud parent, I watched you grow
and felt your growing pains.
I tried to protect you from yourself,
from others. Call it an ulterior motive
if I was always thinking of myself.
I asked you to do things you shouldn't have.
I should have known better.
You wore my bruises, my embarrassments.
Though I accepted the blame, you bore the blows.
From the beginning, Job, you knew your Lot.
You have carried me for so long,
who is the real care-giver, the disabled?
You brought me the world through your senses.
You gave voice to my words:
I taught you the tenses.
I gave you the confidence to explore,
the willingness to continue.
You were my forces, my ground troops,
while I droned overhead on your missions.
We were in this together, or not at all.

I put you through hell: you gave me heaven.
I'd like nothing more than to be forgiven.
Shall I give you all my last accounting?

              ****

Skin sometimes a scratch gave me such pleasure!
I pampered you with creams and lotions:
I wanted you softer, to smell better.
You kept me contained, within myself,
a border challenged but resilient.

Pimples and boils: occasionally conflict
rose to the surface. Scratches and cuts:
wounds of the world, you gave them scabs.
Black and blue were your proud dark colors.
The sun was your nemesis and lover.
You blushed my thoughts and rashly judged,
but protected me through thick and thin.
My bodyguard, my Achilles shield.

Toes I admit it: I took you for granted
and never gave you a second thought,
till you stubbed my path
and I stumbled. I enjoyed you most
when you kneaded the sand on the beach.
In these last years by neglect,
you've been getting numb. Sorry.

Feet like tree roots, you let me stand
above the fray yet kept me grounded.
My taxi, my horse, my flying carpet.
You carried me through the dark streets,
the fragrant woods, the long corridors.
You enabled me to stand tall, balanced,
to hold my own in front of others.

Knees what I needed to pray, to climb,
to cushion the coming down.
The well-oiled hinge between here and there.
You put a bounce in my steps,
got me up out of bed every morning.

Legs with you I ran, swam, kicked, jumped—
became a mobile creature, action figure.
You gave me the bicycle, the treadmill,
the chance to change my vistas, the speed

to catch up and overtake, to dawdle.
To walk was a daily divine dance.

Buttocks cushions to rest upon,
occasionally pinched or squeezed.
Where I got slapped when young and naughty.
When I think of all the meals and classes
I made you sit through,
buoyed by your patience, your solace,
your comforting consolation!
You got a bum rap for being an ass.

Penis surely, a man's best friend.
Loyal, stalwart, you stood up when I asked,
or when the urge rose
and proved undeniable.
A stand-in, the baton tasked
to pass on my genes
with each successful surge.
A diamond in the rough,
undercover agent ready
to spring to attention.
No doubt, your role was enviable.
A little too boastful?

Anus exit of detritus,
where I added to the dung heap
of life and washed my hands of it.
To what I could not keep,
you delivered the eviction notice.
There is no shame in your fame.

Internal organs my waste management
and repair shops, where recycling took place
in assembly line fashion.
My bellows and my furnace.

A pipeline of renewable energy.
A city that never slept, a world
unto itself with its own language.
Occasionally I'd hear its syllables,
rumblings of rebellion, murmurings,
always appeased when my gut felt good.

Belly button my ground zero,
where I began living alone.
Once the cord was cut,
there was no turning back:
the shuttle door was closed,
I found myself adrift in space,
challenged to find a kinder
universe, where I could survive
on my own, of my own making.
You were a constant reminder.

Chest no medals were pinned on you,
but I was proud to know
I was made of something solid, thump-able.
The stronghold of my heart, chivalrous
to the core. A headrest par excellence
even the cat recognized.

Back keeping you straight was a mission
I was miserable at, but you shouldered
the extra weight, the baggage I needed
where I was going. I loved lying down
with your imponderable strength.
My bedrock, you were hard to see,
and needed an occasional scratch
or rub to remind me.

Heart indefatigable, yet fragile
as the next breath, the next love.

The internal reactor, hot rods and all,
that powered everything, fast or slow,
and some speeds in between, but never off
kilter. You never took a timeout.
I will make that up to you.

Arms how I embraced the world
and others and brought them close.
What I used to throw and hit
and swing for the fences.
Extending you, I dove
into unknown waters.

Right hand my best man. You signed my name
by proxy. You welcomed
my friends and greeted strangers.
You fussed over me like a butler.
And like a big brother, tended
to your siblings here, combing,
brushing, washing. You could deliver
the big punch. You kept me fed.

Left hand a vice-president,
there to decide if necessary,
an understudy, you'd do in a pinch,
my pinch hitter. A shadow figure,
mimicker, always the younger brother.

Fingers spidery crawlers
tipped with hard shiny shells,
clattering across surfaces, snapping the air,
prying open cavities. My raccoons.
10 little Indians on a pow-wow.
Clasping you together, I made my vows.
You left my imprimatur
on everything I touched.

Neck the stalk on which the bud rests,
bowed in the presence of higher powers.
Through you everything passed inspection.
My liaison with my empire,
a secretary of state keeping peace
with the outlying provinces.

Ears my own stereo system.
Your brought me thunder from lightning,
the sounds of pain and pleasure,
the voice of every creature
voicing its wishes and complaints.
You caught the music from the notes,
the spirit from the scriptures,
the sound of my own heart's beat.
When I closed my eyes,
I was always attuned.

Nose you gave me a head's-up,
a preview of what was coming
down the pike. You added spice
to an unpalatable existence.
Your teamwork with mouth gave me breath.

Mouth it was hard to keep you shut
when I had so much to say.
You expressed my joy and happiness,
gifted those closest with kisses.
You smacked of the marvelous.

Teeth biting, crunching, chewing,
you broke everything down
into manageable bits, parsing food,
mashing in the pit. The work took its toll.
I spent more on you than anything else,
but could hardly afford any downtime.

It meant something to see you dressed in white,
shoulder to shoulder, at attention.
You earned your gold crown,
making the difficult easier to swallow.

Eyes you focused the world in depth
and high definition: I was near-sighted.
Even so, I was captivated
by the moving picture show
of your cable vision. Without you,
I would have had to recreate
every tree and blade of grass
and never known the grandeur of the sky,
the beauty of the women I loved.
Without you, there was no reality
except my fabrications, my fantasy,
which could never match your gifts.
You were a passport full of visas.

Brain a labyrinth of endless wanderings,
a maze of amazement,
the bank vault where I stored my ingots.
Super computer, supreme court chief.
The proverbial riddle, wrapped
in a mystery, inside an enigma.
While I slept, you patrolled,
my 24-hr. security blanket
and secret service. The castle
where I lived under house arrest.
I was sentenced here to life
imprisonment, with no parole;
though I escaped every night,
I submitted to custody
in the morning. General, CEO,
you forged me an identity card
that proved I was who I was. Wasn't I?

****

So I will make the arrangements
to have you cremated properly.
I don't want you mouldering in a box
underground, with a tombstone title.
I will tell them where to spread your ashes.

I could have put this all down in a letter,
but then I'd have had to read it to you.
Why am I talking as if we are two?
Rather, we are halves. You are my better.

Please rest this head in your hands, old you-who.

Aste**risk**

> "The asteroid, bigger than an aircraft carrier, will dart between the Earth and moon Tuesday — the closest encounter by such a huge rock in 35 years."
> –AP (11/7/2011)

That was a close call. Makes you think
how the end came to the dinosaurs.
Once again, we were brought back from the brink
of our innocence by the void outdoors.

That such thugs roam the universe
destined to cause trouble makes one pause
to ponder our fragility, and curse—
our sense of purpose has huge flaws.

How old could it be? Ugly as sin,
born in the interstices of time,
homeless, pulled in a direction
that might circle back on itself like time—

like a bad dream, from which we awaken
forever challenged to forget a threat
that so rocked our sleep that sweat
sopped the skin. What do you feel? Forsaken.

Fashion Designer

"Shall I call you Miss, or Ms., or Mrs.?
Whatever style you derive from clothes,
you look naked, dear, without my kisses."

Blessed is the man who counts his blisses
helping a woman shed all of those
veils—the Miss, the Ms., even the Mrs.—

to show what's underneath (so hot it hisses!)
while she models a more natural pose—
endearing the nakedness he kisses.

Yet, after his share of hits and misses,
trying to learn what every woman knows
of mischief and mystery (<u>and</u> Mrs.

Grundy), he's still left guessing what pisses
her off, how many secrets she'll disclose
to the queries of dear, naked kisses.

So it's back to the drawing board he goes
to fashion women as they metamorphose
from Miss to Ms., and most to Mrs.—
"Dear Nakedness, I'll dress you with my kisses."

Paper Wasps

Over the summer, under the eaves,
the hubbub of paper wasps
continued from breakfast dawn
to dinner dusk. From the kitchen
table window, I watched
arrivals and departures
at their papier-mâché terminal,
wound like the turban
of a cult-thriving swami.
It was buzzing with business.

Making their rounds, their commutes,
coming home and going out
in exploratory searches,
to work, to stores, and even churches,
bringing the nectar fruits
of their labors
back to sustain each subsequent scout:
daily, thus, I regard my neighbors.

Inside, I imagined what was going on:
a queen mother exerting her control
with an aura of significance
over layered hexagonal chambers,
devoutly prepared for the larvae
that were being cloistered there.
When they emerged, the young wasps
were already faithful followers,
preordained in their senses.
Given their paperwork, they flew off.

Is it only about getting things done,
a manufactured magic,
a mindless work ethic,
this ceaseless activity under the sun?
Individuals, whose DNA

is 99.9% the same,
swarming to a meaning they
were destined to proclaim?

Late in the fall, I knocked the nest down.
It lay on the ground like a plundered piñata,
vulnerable to the winter wind and rain.
The queen was as scarce as her crown.

Donations and Gifts

Do we give enough? To the Red Cross,
to Goodwill? To the Salvation Army?
To strangers on the street with their placards
and empty bowls? To the relentless
robotic phone calls and mass mailings?
To our alma mater's annual giving?

The most I've given of myself is blood.
"When I am dead," my mother often said,
"they can have my body." When she was dead,
the hearse hurried round to the hospice door,
whisking her off to a medical school.
The dead give everything to the living,

and don't expect anything in return.
One day a small plastic box arrived
unannounced—heavy, with a personal
handwritten note, from a faraway place:
how the postman brought me my mother back.
Charity is a form of thanksgiving.

Penny Thoughts

Scooped from my pocket,
you make me realize,
by coin-cidence,
how time is loosely spent.
We were minted in the same year:
a wheat cent and a baby boomer.
Awash in the world,
we lost our luster
hobnobbing
with the masses,
often nickel and dimed.
At times, jailed in a jar,
you saved your freedom
for a charitable cause.
How many debts have you paid?
How many dollars broken?
What was wished on you,
and where and why?
Did it ever come true?
Hard to imagine such a small thing—
one might say "insignificant"—
could make everything
and everyone
count.
Our shared destiny
is to keep circulating,
making change,
defining the difference.

Graybeard

My wife is still waiting to see my face.
Maybe tomorrow I will shave my beard,
which I've renewed (like vows) for forty years.

The outlines of my features she must trace
with her hands. Admittedly, it feels weird.
So my smile is more guarded than my peers'.

Is it laziness before the mirror
in the morning? Something I won't reveal?
The cumulative savings that I've banked

in time—and skin kept from the razor—
are part of it. But I've nothing to conceal.
These acts of selflessness are daily thanked.

What does someone need to know to believe
a man shines behind his growing shadow?

Heron Waiting (photograph by Mark Gardner)

> *"They also serve who only stand and wait."*
> —John Milton

Pier-less, the old piles seem to bob and float.
The day is running fast after the light.
The water lies unwakened by a boat.
On his outpost, the heron first turns right,
then swivels to the left. He hones his gaze.
Before him loom mountain and island shapes
that have been the nexus of his days,
the domain of his nights. Here, he escapes.

The photographer has gone, and we suppose
the bird still holds his one-legged yoga pose,
and becomes his own photographer now.
He waits—it's not his nature to coerce—
to see what happens next, and to allow
himself the patience of the universe.

In Sickness and In Health

The path was wide
enough for two.
So side-by-side
I walked with you,
my arm around your waist.

When it grew narrow,
you hooked my elbow—
then single file
for a while
we paced.

Your hand on my shoulder
as we got older
still felt secure,
as we faced
the fastest future.

Though we raced
as fast
as we could, the past
grew faster. To help you stand,
I grabbed your hand.

When you fell behind,
I chased
back my steps to see.
Never mind
me,

you said.
Go ahead.

Leaves

Clenched like fists at the ends of branches,
a few leaves remain recalcitrant
above the freezing ground.

The autumn was loud with their protests
in festive reds, oranges, and yellows:
their cause was legion in the woods.

But across the lawns in the neighborhood
casualties began to mount.
The fallen were herded into piles

by the curb for the township trucks.
Blowers rounded up the stragglers.
Soon winter winds scoured the bare limbs

of the trees till they were skeletons
shaking and clattering in their palsy.
A percussive beat hardened the landscape.

Now only a white barrenness molds
the flowerbeds, the riff-raff evergreens.
A numbing cold has choked all colors.

What is the point of hanging on—
or the obstacle to letting go—
when everything else is gone?

Dividing by Zero

Life juggles constants and variables
through a set of basic operations.

1 divided by 1 is 1.
This proves identity:
each child is the quotient of his parents—
a whole, real entity.

1 plus -1 is 0.
Aristophanes said as much
in the *Symposium*:
'positive' and 'negative'
are merely terms of gender;
Eros directs their combination.

1 times 1 times 1 times 1 . . . is 1.
The solipsistic man
can never get beyond himself.

Old age is a fraction;
senility, an irrational number.
i is the square root of -1:
the impossible dream
each man harbors
under his own roof.

1 minus 1 is 0.
At times, we take back what we said.
Death follows our lead
and double-deals.

3.14159265 is pi,
approximately.
But it is enough to see
our circle of friends
divided by our reach
is always constant.

Days are degrees
of a sine curve.
We take turns
on its roller coaster.

The asymptote is the rope
some men climb in search of God,
plotting, knot by knot, their approach.

If n equals any positive number,
then n divided by zero
equals infinity.
Multiply both sides by zero:
n equals infinity times zero.
How else to calculate
the creation of the universe
by an infinite power
out of nothing?

J**ohn** recently retired after 35 years in the Dept. of Rare Books and Special Collections of Princeton University Library, where he was head of manuscripts processing and then, for the last 15 years, curator of historic maps. He has written a number of works on cartography, including *Strait Through: Magellan to Cook and the Pacific*; *First X, Then Y, Now Z: An Introduction to Landmark Thematic Maps*; and *Nova Caesarea: A Cartographic Record of the Garden State, 1666-1888*. These have extensive website versions. He has written poems for most of his life, and, in the 1970s, he attended the Writing Program of Syracuse University, where his mentors were poets W. D. Snodgrass and Philip Booth. No doubt, in subtle ways, they have bookended his approach to poems. John has traveled widely, preferring remote, natural settings, and is addicted to kayaking and hiking. His *Waypoints* (Seattle, Pleasure Boat Studio), a collection of place poems, appeared in 2017.

Twenty Questions suggests that a poet is well-served by a journalist's curiosity—the who, what, when, where, why (and how)—so that it is natural that he ask questions. About time, and love, himself, and nature. Once you start, it's hard to stop. After John's *Twenty Questions*, you'll want to ask your own.

www.ingramcontent.com/pod-product-compliance
Lightning Source LLC
LaVergne TN
LVHW041504070426
835507LV00012B/1324